路得

「智慧的話」叢書

Ruth

(Words of Wisdom Series)

香港聖經公會
HONG KONG BIBLE SOCIETY

路得（智慧的話叢書）

出 版 者： **香港聖經公會**

　　　　香港九龍尖沙咀漆咸道南 67 號安年大廈 902 室

　　　　電話：(852) 2368 5147　　　傳真：(852) 2311 0167

　　　　網址：www.hkbs.org.hk　　電郵：info@hkbs.org.hk

版　　次：二〇〇九年十一月初版

　　　　二〇一三年十月三版

編　　號：RCU / GNT690P−WOW04

國際書號：978 962 293 133 6

Ruth (Words of Wisdom Series)

HONG KONG BIBLE SOCIETY

Room 902, Oriental Centre, 67 Chatham Road South

Tsimshatsui, Kowloon, Hong Kong

Tel : (852) 2368 5147　　　Fax : (852) 2311 0167

Website : www.hkbs.org.hk　　Email : info@hkbs.org.hk

First Printing, November 2009

Third Printing, October 2013

Code No. RCU / GNT690P−WOW04

ISBN 978 962 293 133 6

Chinese Scripture: Revised Chinese Union Version © 2006, 2010 Hong Kong Bible Society

English Scripture: Good News Bible

Illustrations & other materials © Hong Kong Bible Society

This edition copyright © 2009 Hong Kong Bible Society

「**智慧的話**」叢書乃取材自新舊約聖經，內容以活潑可愛的圖畫將聖經裏的教訓生動地表達出來，目的是提高小孩子對聖經的興趣和了解，啓發他們思考聖經與他們生活的關係。

「智慧的話」叢書是一系列的聖經圖畫故事。書內備有關於背景之資料及思考問題，期望小孩子讀後留下深刻的印象。書後附有參考經文，採自和合本修訂版。本書適合作教材或輔助讀物之用。

"**Words of Wisdom**" series presents stories from the Old and New Testaments at a level that children can read for themselves. It contains bright and attractive pictures to help bring out the teaching of the Scriptures. The aim of the series is to make the Bible come alive to children so that they will become more interested in its message. Then they can see how valuable it is for their own lives.

"Words of Wisdom" series provides background information for each story for parents to read. There are also questions to think about, in the hope that the message of the stories will be remembered. At the back of each booklet is the Bible text for each story taken from the Good News Bible. These story books may be used as teaching materials in Sunday Schools as well as at home. They may also be used to share with friends who do not yet know about God's Good News.

拿娥米和她的丈夫住在以色列的伯利恆，他們有兩個兒子。

Naomi and her husband lived in Bethlehem, a town in Israel. They had two sons.

以色列國發生了饑荒，沒有東西吃。他們就搬到外國去。

Because there was a famine in the land of Israel, they had nothing to eat. Naomi and her family moved to another country, Moab.

後來，拿娥米的丈夫死在那裏。拿娥米的兒子長大了。他們和當地的女子結婚。

Later on, Naomi's husband died. Naomi's two sons grew up. They married Moabite girls.

約十年後，拿娥米的兩個兒子死了，只剩下她和兩個媳婦。

About ten years, Naomi's two sons also died. Naomi lived with her two daughters-in-law.

不久，拿娥米對兩個媳婦說：「我要回伯利恆去，因為那裏有
食物。你們留在這裏，因為這是你們的家。」其中一個媳婦路
得說：「婆婆！你到哪裏，我也到哪裏；你的神就是我的神。
請讓我跟你一起回去！」於是她們一起回伯利恆去。

After some time, Naomi said to them, "I want to go back to Bethlehem. There is food now. You may stay here in Moab because it is your home." One daughter-in-law, Ruth, said to Naomi, "I want to go with you. Your people are my people. Your God is my God." So they went to Bethlehem.

她們到達伯利恆。那時正是收割的時候。全城的人都忙着工作。他們看見路得和拿娥米，都很高興。

They arrived in Bethlehem at harvest time. Everyone was busy gathering the harvest. They were very happy when they saw Ruth and Naomi.

有一天，路得到田裏去。她撿拾留給窮人的麥穗。她來到波
阿斯的麥田。波阿斯是拿娥米的親戚。

One day Ruth went to the fields. She gathered grain which the workers left behind for the poor people and widows to collect. Ruth went to the field of a man called Boaz. Boaz was a relative of Naomi.

波阿斯看見路得，就問工人說：「那女子是誰？」工人回答說：「她就是跟拿娥米一起回來的外國女子路得。」波阿斯吩咐工人：「多留些麥穗給路得撿拾吧！」

Boaz saw Ruth and asked, "Who is that foreign girl?" The workers told him it was Naomi's daughter-in-law who came with her from Moab. Boaz told the workers "Leave lots of grain for her to gather."

波阿斯請路得留在他的田裏工作。他說：「我的工人會好好待你。他們會分一點東西給你吃。」

Boaz asked Ruth to work in his field. He said, "My workers will take care of you very well. They will share their food and drink with you."

傍晚，路得把撿到的麥子帶回家。拿娥米看見這許多的麥子，非常高興。她對路得說：「神在幫助我們。你要每天到波阿斯的田裏去工作，因為他是我們的親戚。」

Each evening Ruth took grain home. Naomi was also very pleased. She said to Ruth, "God is helping us. Go to Boaz's field every day. He is one of my relatives."

波阿斯對伯利恆的人說：「我不願意路得和拿娥米孤單地生活。我要好好照顧她們。我要娶路得做妻子。」於是波阿斯和路得結了婚。

Boaz said to the people of Bethlehem, "I do not want Naomi and Ruth to be so lonely. I shall take care of them. I would like to marry Ruth." So Boaz and Ruth were married.

後來，路得和波阿斯生了一個兒子。他們給他起名叫俄備得。拿娥米快樂地照顧他。伯利恆的婦女說：「神太好了！他使拿娥米的家又有了兒子。願他大有名聲。」

Afterwards, Boaz and Ruth had a son. They called him Obed. Naomi was happy to take care of him. The women in Bethlehem all said, "God is so good. He has given Naomi's family another son. May he become famous!"

參考經文
Reference

以利米勒全家遷往摩押

　　士師統治的時候，國中有饑荒。在猶大的伯利恆，有一個人帶着妻子和兩個兒子往摩押地去寄居。這人名叫以利米勒，他的妻子名叫拿娥米；他兩個兒子，一個名叫瑪倫，一個名叫基連，都是猶大伯利恆的以法他人。他們到了摩押地，就住在那裏。後來拿娥米的丈夫以利米勒死了，剩下她和兩個兒子。兩個兒子娶了摩押女子，一個名叫俄珥巴，第二個名叫路得，在那裏住了約有十年。瑪倫和基連二人也死了，剩下拿娥米，沒有丈夫，也沒有兒子。

路得跟拿娥米回伯利恆

　　拿娥米與兩個媳婦起身，要從摩押地回去，因為她在摩押地聽見耶和華眷顧自己的百姓，賜糧食給他們。她和兩個媳婦就起行，離開所住的地方，上路回猶大地去。拿娥米對兩個媳婦說：「你們各自回娘家去吧！願耶和華恩待你們，像你們待已故的人和我一樣。願耶和華使你們各自在新的丈夫家中得歸宿！」

路得記 1．1-9

路得說：
「不要勸我離開你，
轉去不跟隨你。
你往哪裏去，
我也往哪裏去；
你在哪裏住，
我也在哪裏住；
你的百姓就是我的百姓；
你的神就是我的神。
你死在哪裏，

Elimelech and His Family Move to Moab

Long ago, in the days before Israel had a king, there was a famine in the land. So a man named Elimelech, who belonged to the clan of Ephrath and who lived in Bethlehem in Judah, went with his wife Naomi and their two sons Mahlon and Chilion to live for a while in the country of Moab. While they were living there, Elimelech died, and Naomi was left alone with her two sons, who married Moabite women, Orpah and Ruth. About ten years later Mahlon and Chilion also died, and Naomi was left all alone, without husband or sons.

Naomi and Ruth Return to Bethlehem

Some time later Naomi heard that the Lord had blessed his people by giving them good crops; so she got ready to leave Moab with her daughters-in-law. They started out together to go back to Judah, but on the way she said to them, "Go back home and stay with your mothers. May the Lord be as good to you as you have been to me and to those who have died. And may the Lord make it possible for each of you to marry again and have a home."

Ruth 1.1-9

But Ruth answered, "Don't ask me to leave you! Let me go with you. Wherever you go, I will go; wherever you live, I will live. Your people will be my people, and your God will be my God. Wherever you die, I will die, and that is where I will be buried. May the Lord's worst punishment come upon me if I let anything but death separate me from you!"

When Naomi saw that Ruth was determined to go with her, she said nothing more.

They went on until they came to Bethlehem. When they arrived, the whole town became excited, and the women there exclaimed, "Is this really Naomi?"

"Don't call me Naomi," she answered; "call me Marah, because Almighty God has made my life bitter. When I left here, I had plenty, but the Lord has brought me back without a thing. Why call me Naomi when the Lord Almighty has condemned me and sent me trouble?"

This, then, was how Naomi came back from Moab with Ruth, her Moabite daughter-in-law. When they arrived in Bethlehem, the barley harvest was just beginning.

Ruth Works in the Field of Boaz

Naomi had a relative named Boaz, a rich and influential man who belonged to the family of her husband Elimelech. One day Ruth said to Naomi, "Let me go to the fields to gather the grain that the harvest workers leave. I am sure to find someone who will let me work with him."

Naomi answered, "Go ahead, daughter."

So Ruth went out to the fields and walked behind the workers, picking up the heads of grain which they left. It so happened that she was in a field that belonged to Boaz.

Some time later Boaz himself arrived from Bethlehem and greeted the workers. "The Lord be with you!" he said.

"The Lord bless you!" they answered.

Boaz asked the man in charge, "Who is

我也死在哪裏，葬在哪裏。

只有死能使你我分離；

不然，願耶和華重重懲罰我！」

拿娥米見路得決意要跟自己去，就不再對她說甚麼了。

於是二人同行，來到伯利恆。她們到了伯利恆，全城因她們騷動起來。婦女們說：「這是拿娥米嗎？」拿娥米對她們說：

「不要叫我拿娥米，

要叫我瑪拉，

因為全能者使我受盡了苦。

我滿滿地出去，

耶和華使我空空地回來。

耶和華使我受苦，

全能者降禍於我。

你們為何還叫我拿娥米呢？」

拿娥米從摩押地回來了，她的媳婦摩押女子路得跟她在一起。她們到了伯利恆，正是開始收割大麥的時候。

路得在田間遇見波阿斯

拿娥米有一個親戚，是她丈夫以利米勒本族的人，名叫波阿斯，是個大財主。摩押女子路得對拿娥米說：「讓我到田裏去拾取麥穗，我在誰的眼中蒙恩，就跟在誰的身後。」拿娥米說：「女兒啊，你去吧！」路得就去了。她來到田間，在收割的人身後拾取麥穗。她恰巧來到以利米勒本族的人波阿斯那塊田裏。看哪，波阿斯正從伯利恆來，對收割的人說：「願耶和華與你們同在！」他們對他說：「願耶和華賜福給你！」波阿斯對監督收割的僕人說：「那是誰家的女子？」監督收割的僕人回答說:「她是摩押女子,跟隨拿娥米從摩押地回來的。她說:『請你容許我拾取麥穗,在收割的人身後撿禾捆中掉落的麥穗。』她就來了,從早晨直到如今,除了在屋子裏坐一會兒,她都留在這裏。」

波阿斯對路得說:「女兒啊,聽我說,不要到別人田裏去拾取麥穗,也不要離開這裏,要緊跟着我的女僕們。你要看好我的僕人正在哪塊田收割,就跟着女僕們去。我已經吩咐僕人不可侵犯你。你渴了,可以到水缸那裏喝僕人打來的水。」路得就臉伏於地叩拜,對他說:「我既是外邦女子,怎麼會在你眼中蒙恩,使你這樣照顧我呢?」波阿斯回答她說:「自從你丈夫死後,凡你向婆婆所行的,以及你離開父母和你的出生地,到素不相識的百姓中,這些事人都告訴我了。願耶和華照你所行的報償你。你來投靠在耶和華——以色列神的翅膀下,願你滿得他的報償。」路得說:「我主啊,願我在你眼前蒙恩。我雖然不及你的一個婢女,你還安慰我,對你的婢女說關心的話。」

吃飯的時候,波阿斯對路得說:「你到這裏來吃些餅,把你的一塊蘸在醋裏。」路得就在收割的人旁邊坐下。波阿斯把烘了的穗子遞給她。她吃飽了,還有剩餘的。她又起來拾取麥穗,波阿斯吩咐僕人說:「她即使在禾捆中拾取麥穗,也不可羞辱她。你們還要從捆裏抽一些出來,留給她拾取,不可責備她。」

這樣,路得在田間拾取麥穗,直到

that young woman?"

The man answered, "She is the foreigner who came back from Moab with Naomi. She asked me to let her follow the workers and gather grain. She has been working since early morning and has just now stopped to rest for a while under the shelter."

Then Boaz said to Ruth, "Let me give you some advice. Don't gather grain anywhere except in this field. Work with the women here; watch them to see where they are reaping and stay with them. I have ordered my men not to molest you. And whenever you are thirsty, go and drink from the water jars that they have filled."

Ruth bowed down with her face touching the ground, and said to Boaz, "Why should you be so concerned about me? Why should you be so kind to a foreigner?"

Boaz answered, "I have heard about everything that you have done for your mother-in-law since your husband died. I know how you left your father and mother and your own country and how you came to live among a people you had never known before. May the Lord reward you for what you have done. May you have a full reward from the Lord God of Israel, to whom you have come for protection!"

Ruth answered, "You are very kind to me, sir. You have made me feel better by speaking gently to me, even though I am not the equal of one of your servants."

At mealtime Boaz said to Ruth, "Come and have a piece of bread, and dip it in the sauce." So she sat with the workers, and Boaz passed some roasted grain to her. She ate until she was satisfied, and she still had some food left over. After she had left to go and gather grain, Boaz ordered the workers, "Let her gather grain even where the bundles are lying, and don't say anything to stop her. Besides that, pull out some heads of grain from the bundles and leave them for her to pick up."

So Ruth gathered grain in the field until evening, and when she had beaten it out, she found she had nearly twenty-five pounds. She took the grain back into town and showed her mother-in-law how much she had gathered. She also gave her the food left over from the meal. Naomi asked her, "Where did you gather all this grain today? Whose field have you been working in? May God bless the man who took an interest in you!"

So Ruth told Naomi that she had been working in a field belonging to a man named Boaz.

"May the Lord bless Boaz!" Naomi exclaimed. "The Lord always keeps his promises to the living and the dead." And she went on, "That man is a close relative of ours, one of those responsible for taking care of us."

Ruth 1.16—2.20

Then Boaz said to the leaders and all the others there, "You are all witnesses today that I have bought from Naomi everything that belonged to Elimelech and to his sons Chilion and Mahlon. In addition, Ruth the Moabite, Mahlon's widow, becomes my wife. This will keep the property in the dead man's family, and his family line will continue among his people and in his hometown. You are witnesses to this today."

The leaders and the others said, "Yes, we are witnesses. May the Lord make your wife become like Rachel and Leah, who bore many children to Jacob. May you become rich in the clan of Ephrath and famous in Bethlehem. May the children that the Lord will give you by this young woman make your family like the family of Perez, the son of Judah and Tamar."

Boaz and His Descendants

So Boaz took Ruth home as his wife. The Lord blessed her, and she became pregnant and had a son. The women said to Naomi, "Praise the Lord! He has given you a grandson today to take care of you. May the boy become famous in Israel! Your daughter-in-law loves you, and has done

晚上。她把所拾取的麥穗打了約有一伊法的大麥。路得把所拾取的帶進城去給婆婆看，又把她吃飽了所剩的拿出來，給了婆婆。婆婆問她說：「你今日在哪裏拾取麥穗？在哪裏做工呢？願那照顧你的得福。」路得告訴婆婆，她在誰那裏做工，說：「我今日在一個名叫波阿斯的人那裏做工。」拿娥米對媳婦說：「願那人蒙耶和華賜福，因為他不斷地恩待活人死人。」拿娥米又對她說：「那人是我本族的人，是一個可以贖我們產業的至親。」

路得記 1．16—2．20

波阿斯對長老和所有在場的百姓說：「你們今日都是證人；凡屬以利米勒，以及基連和瑪倫的，我都從拿娥米手中買下來了。我也娶瑪倫的妻子摩押女子路得，好讓死人可以在產業上留名，免得他的名在本族本鄉的城門中消失了。你們今日都是證人。」在城門坐着的所有百姓和長老說：「我們都是證人。願耶和華使進你家的這女子，像建立以色列家的拉結和利亞二人一樣。又願你在以法他得亨通，在伯利恆有名聲。願耶和華從這年輕女子賜你後裔，使你的家像她瑪從猶大所生法勒斯的家一樣。」

大衛的家譜

於是，波阿斯娶了路得為妻，與她同房。耶和華使她懷孕生了一個兒子。婦女們對拿娥米說：「耶和華是應當稱頌的！因為他今日沒有使你斷絕可以贖產業的至親。願這孩子在以色列中得名聲。

more for you than seven sons. And now she has given you a grandson, who will bring new life to you and give you security in your old age." Naomi took the child, held him close, and took care of him.

The women of the neighborhood named the boy Obed. They told everyone, "A son has been born to Naomi!"

Obed became the father of Jesse, who was the father of David.

This is the family line from Perez to David: Perez, Hezron, Ram, Amminadab, Nahshon, Salmon, Boaz, Obed, Jesse, David.

Ruth 4.9-22

他必振奮你的精神，奉養你的晚年，因為他是愛慕你的媳婦所生的。有這樣的媳婦，比有七個兒子更好！」拿娥米接過孩子來，抱在懷中撫養他。鄰居的婦人給孩子起名，說：「拿娥米得了一個孩子了！」她們就給他起名叫俄備得。俄備得是耶西的父親，是大衛的祖父。

這是法勒斯的後代：法勒斯生希斯崙；希斯崙生蘭；蘭生亞米拿達；亞米拿達生拿順；拿順生撒門；撒門生波阿斯；波阿斯生俄備得；俄備得生耶西；耶西生大衛。

路得記 4．9-22